The Beatles: Unseen

John Howard

Penguin Books

PENGUIN BOOKS

Published by the Penguin Group
Penguin Books Ltd, 27 Wrights Lane, London W8 5TZ, England
Penguin Books USA Inc., 375 Hudson Street, New York, New York 10014, USA
Penguin Books Australia Ltd, Ringwood, Victoria, Australia
Penguin Books Canada Ltd, 10 Alcorn Avenue, Toronto, Ontario, Canada M4V 3B2
Penguin Books (NZ) Ltd, 182–190 Wairau Road, Auckland 10, New Zealand

Penguin Books Ltd, Registered Offices: Harmondsworth, Middlesex, England

First published 1996
10 9 8 7 6 5 4 3 2 1

Typeset in Monotype Grotesque
Designed in QuarkXpress on an Apple Macintosh
Printed in England by Butler & Tanner Ltd, Frome and London

Let Me Introduce to You ...

Still high from touring the Taj Mahal by moonlight with Jackie Kennedy, then appearing as an Egyptian trumpeter in Rome in the epic *Cleopatra* and getting to know its stars, Elizabeth Taylor and Richard Burton, better than I know myself, I needed an excuse to visit an ailing relative in Australia. John, Paul, George and Ringo came to my rescue ...

On 11 June 1964 the three moptops arrived in torrential rain at Sydney airport, via Darwin. Welcome platforms had been set up on the airport tarmac and the Beatles were driven from the plane to the terminal on the back of trucks so that they could wave to their fans. Jimmy Nicol, the 'temporary Beatle' who was sitting in for Ringo Starr until he'd recovered from tonsillitis, stared out in wonder from under a big umbrella as the fans stood screaming for joy. Raindrops mingled with tears as they sang 'Yeah, Yeah, Yeah!'. I began my odyssey with a Leica M3 then changed to a Rolleiflex and various Canon cameras.

The day before the Beatles' arrival I had booked myself a small suite for £36 a day at the tiny Sheraton Hotel in Macleay Street. That night I threw a twenty-second birthday party for Paul. I'd asked friends Des and Jan Noonan to help out. When the fab 'three' showed up, John was soon twisting, if not shouting, and George, a little dazed, was clutching a gift from a fan: a felt-padded toy kangaroo. Paul made a fuss over the female guests before turning his attentions to the strawberry sponge birthday

cake that Jan had made in the shape of Australia and decorated with chocolate koala bears and candles.

I would not meet Ringo until he joined his mates in Melbourne, at a party I threw at the Southern Cross Hotel, which was also attended by cast members from *Camelot* and the Oz musical *Sentimental Bloke*. (Paul Daneman, who played Arthur in *Camelot*, would appear two years later with John Lennon in *How I Won the War*.) As Ringo had just returned from his convalescence, the conversation turned to his tonsils. 'They have to come out sometime,' said Ringo. 'I can't have them stuffing up my throat. George wants me to raffle them.'

'But they're squirmy, horrible things,' declared Paul.

'Perhaps they'll sell them at the hospital,' added George.

'They can't do that,' said John. 'There won't be much left of Ringo after his tonsils are gone. If the hospital were to do a raffle, you could sue them, Ringo! After all, they're your tonsils.'

I flew to Brisbane with the Beatles and planned another party with the help of Patricia Nelki and David Fleay, who ran the David Fleay Fauna Reserve. The VIP guests were a kangaroo, a koala bear, and a dingo puppy called 'Ringo'. Ringo himself had wanted to meet some real Australians, and it was kindly arranged by the Methodist Mission for three aboriginal sisters, Mona, Joan and Amy Smith, to attend.

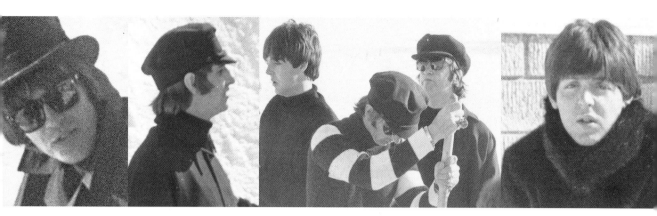

They arrived smartly dressed in woollen twin-sets and accompanied by chaperones. I think Ringo had expected them to turn up in tribal gear. The party took place at the aptly named Lennon's Hotel, about which John commented, 'I knew my relatives were rich, but I didn't know they owned a bloomin' hotel.'

In Brisbane the Beatles were pelted with eggs by male fans, perhaps jealous of the distraction the fab four were causing amongst their girlfriends. 'In our country we usually have eggs for *breakfast*,' Ringo said. One of the egg-throwing ringleaders commented, 'We just wanted to see if they could take it.'

'Of course we could take it, but I like mine scrambled on toast. The other three like theirs fried – right, George?' replied Ringo.

Back in Europe, in March 1965, I photographed the Beatles in the ski resort of Obertauern, Austria, used for the snow scenes in *Help!.* It was in Obertauern that we lucky few members of the public were the first to hear 'Ticket to Ride'. We skied for days to the wonderful booming rhythm of the song, which Dick Lester used as a soundtrack for filming. It is impossible now for me to see snow without thinking of 'Ticket to Ride'. The intimacy of the village meant that I had more opportunity to interact directly with the band, and I felt I'd finally 'arrived' on the day George asked me to help him hide his skis so they wouldn't get stolen while he was having lunch.

It was on 8 October 1966 that I trekked through the desert of Almería, Spain, to

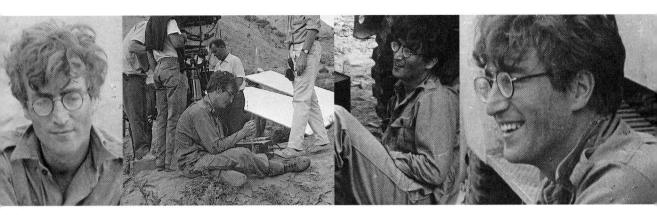

meet John Lennon on another Dick Lester set, this time for the anti-war film *How I Won the War*. (Dick, who had directed *A Hard Day's Night* and *Help!*, was already a well-established director of zany comedies, having filmed, amongst others, comic legends Buster Keaton and Groucho Marx.) John was playing the role of Musketeer Corporal Gripweed in the movie, yet the other three 'musketeers' in his life were elsewhere, and he'd obviously grown a bit lonely. I was flattered upon my arrival by the warm welcome John gave me and by the surprise he showed at my visit.

As a link to the Beatles I think I must have represented to John the adulation he'd been enjoying for the past three years. He did not have the usual security blanket of his three constant companions, and for a couple of days I filled that role. If you like, the role lasted for as long as it takes to shoot a couple of hundred pictures at one five-hundredth of a second each.

John never posed. I had to go after the shots.

From this group of photos came those of which Dick Lester has said, 'They are the best pictures that exist of John Lennon.' It is a series of which I am particularly proud.

I dedicate this book with humble thanks to the great twentieth-century peace-maker, John Ono Lennon, and to his fellow immortals, Paul, George and Ringo.

John Howard

John Howard worked as a Newsweek *correspondent in 1962, covering Jacqueline Kennedy's tour of Pakistan. He was also hired in India by United Press/Fox Movietone News as a cameraman on the same tour. As a writer and photographer he has specialized in covering celebrity personalities, in particular Elizabeth Taylor, the Kennedys and the Beatles.*

He has photographed and interviewed any number of twentieth-century legends, from Astaire, Bardot, Crawford, Davis and Dietrich to De Niro, Eastwood, Wayne, Welch and Zappa.

Something to Get Hung About

The Beatles liked to enjoy themselves without people making a fuss. At the parties I threw over the years I made sure that was how it was. Each time, having extended the fab four an invitation, I never promised anyone they would show up. But luckily for me at least one, and often two, three or all four, always did. In the picture to the right, George autographs the plaster cast of a future 'Apple Scruff', the name he later gave to the female fans who patrolled up and down outside the Apple office at No. 3 Savile Row. Many Beatle autographs were in fact signed by the fifth, sixth and seventh Beatles: roadies Neil Aspinall and Mal Evans, and press officer Derek Taylor. They would take on the duty whenever writer's cramp set in for the actual four. Flying with them from Sydney to Brisbane, and later Genoa to Milan, I saw the Beatles' autograph machine at work. George would say, 'Derek, it's your turn to do mine,' and naturally enough they'd sometimes forget who was who. Probably the most valuable Beatle signatures were the ones George signed for Paul, Ringo signed for John ... No matter which of the seven, it did not make the autographs any less official.

My first Beatles party, June 1964.
Jan Noonan's cake and George's
toy kangaroo sit idly as John
delights the crowd. Jan was five
months pregnant at the time.

From left to right: Lorraine Garness-Sydall, now a doll-making granny in Colorado, at the time a TV songstress; Lynette Hutch, a pharmacist; Karen Richter, of New Guinea, to whom Paul confided that, in addition to the cake shaped like Australia, he'd been gifted with red silk pajamas; Barbara West, who'd recently been widowed and who was cheered up by the three moptops.

'You look just like my wife Cynthia,' John Lennon told Nancy Harloff, the blonde behind George. In fact, Nancy, who worked as a telephone operator for a local cordial factory, looked more like Brigitte Bardot. John fancied the French star and wanted Cynthia to sculpt herself to look more like her.

(Jan Noonan is to the left of Paul.)
John had brought his aunt Mimi to
Australia, but she decided not to
attend the party so that the boys
could let their hair down ...

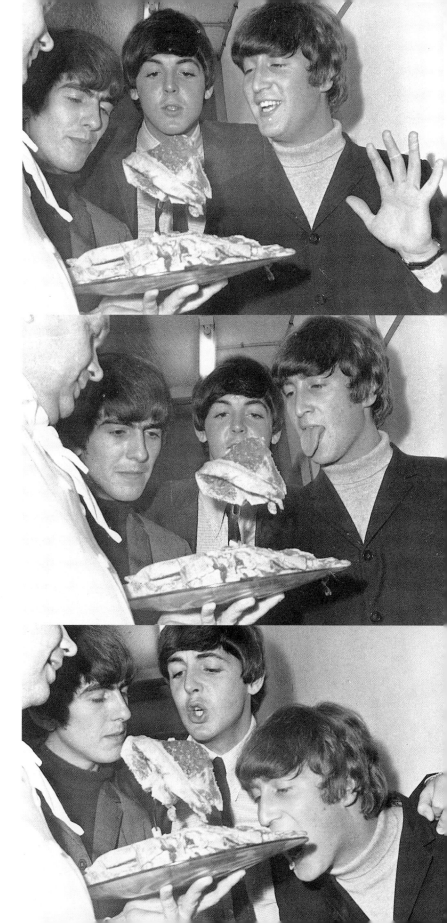

The chef at the Sheraton gave George, John and now-famous-vegetarian Paul a chance to approve these raw rump steaks before making them sizzle.

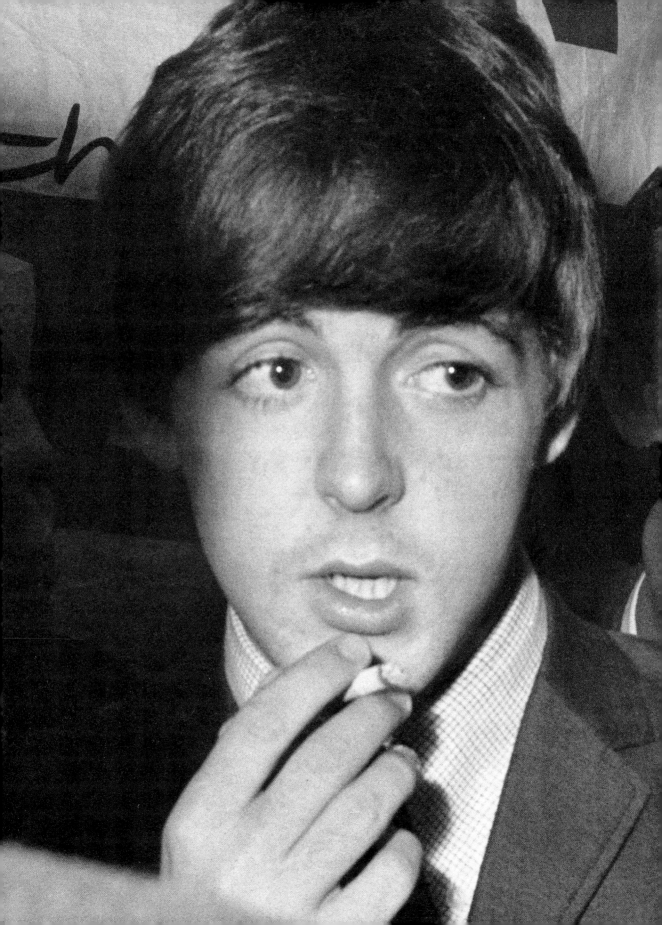

The 'temporary Beatle', Jimmy Nicol, enjoying one of his twelve days of fame, in Sydney. Jimmy was paid £250 a week and received an inscribed gold watch before returning to virtual obscurity. Note the too-short jacket sleeves of his suit, which belonged to Ringo.

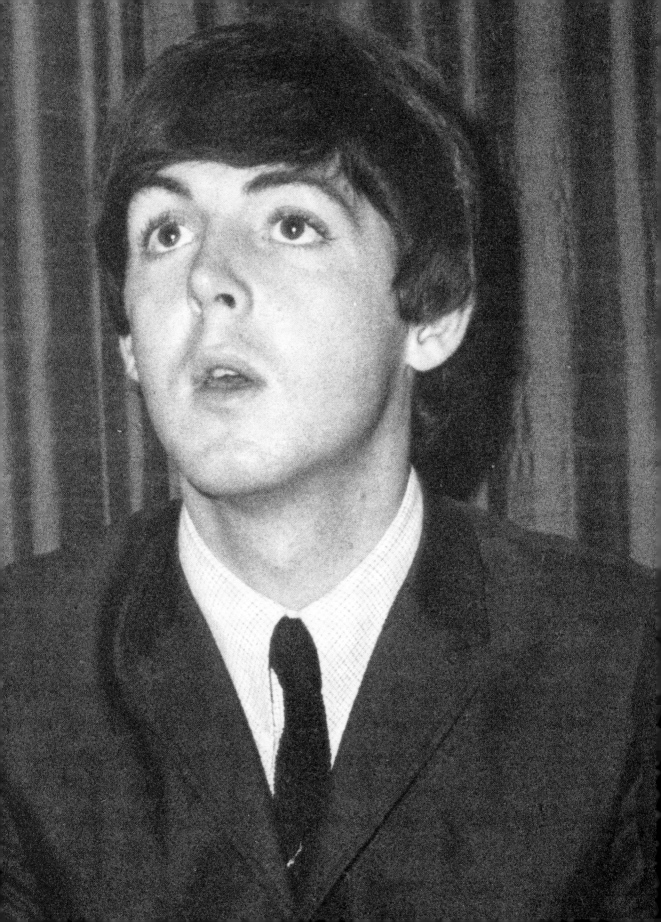

No, not Buckingham Palace
but the 'throne room' of the
Colombo Hotel in Genoa.
These are some of my favourite
shots (I still have the hotel
ashtray). The Beatles' manager,
Brian Epstein, stands beside
John. Next to Brian is Wendy
Hansen, Brian's secretary and
sometime aide to individual
Beatles. She'd previously worked
as a secretary to JFK.

The Beatles were at their ease, but the Italian newsmen who were supposed to barrage them with questions seemed some- what overawed and the queries were slow in coming.

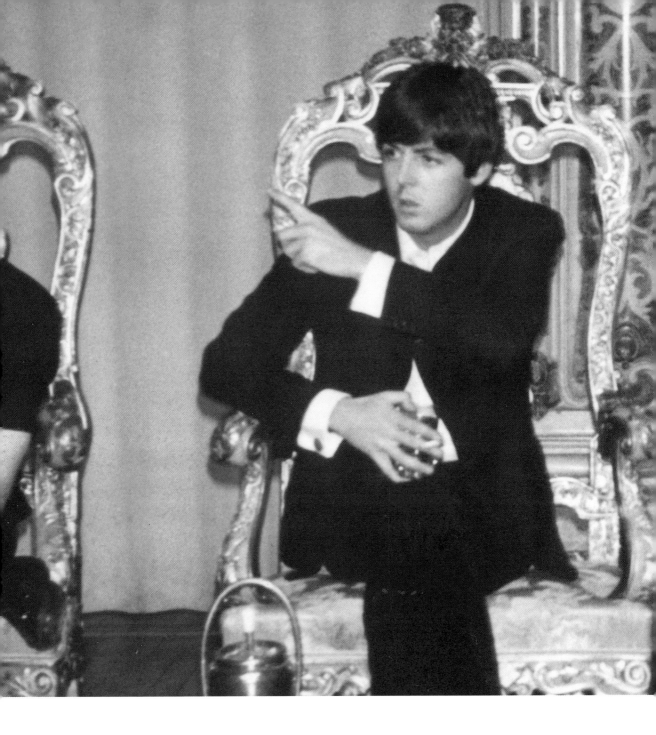

'That's enough of those naughty questions. We won't have any of that Dolce Vita *business* here,' said Paul. 'We are used to family audiences.' This was in response to a question to George, who was asked if it was true that he'd been swimming in the Mediterranean in the buff.

'Me swim naked?' George replied.
'I'm always at least covered in goose
pimples.'

On the Long and Winding Road

Italy is sometimes slow to pick up on fads. When I travelled there with the Beatles on tour, I was amazed to find some of their concerts were not fully subscribed. I think the boys were a bit taken aback as well. At their performance in Genoa, which did not start until 10 p.m., their audience was ninety per cent male. In Genoa, in 1965, teenage girls simply did not go out at night.

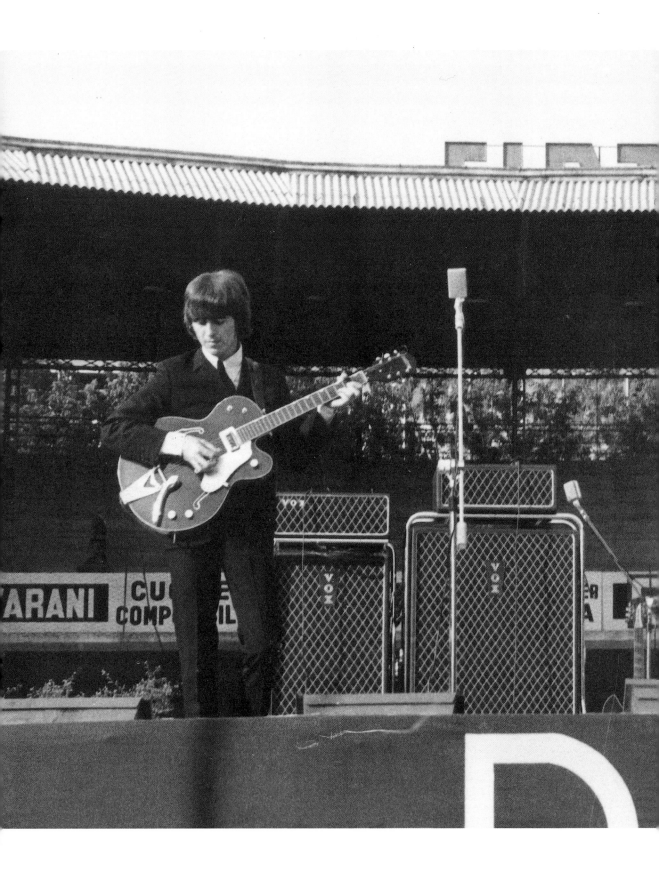

Milan audiences were a little snobbish, as shown by these photographs of an afternoon concert at the Velodrome cycling stadium, where the entire back grandstand was empty. Word of mouth did have an effect though, and the rest of the shows were packed.

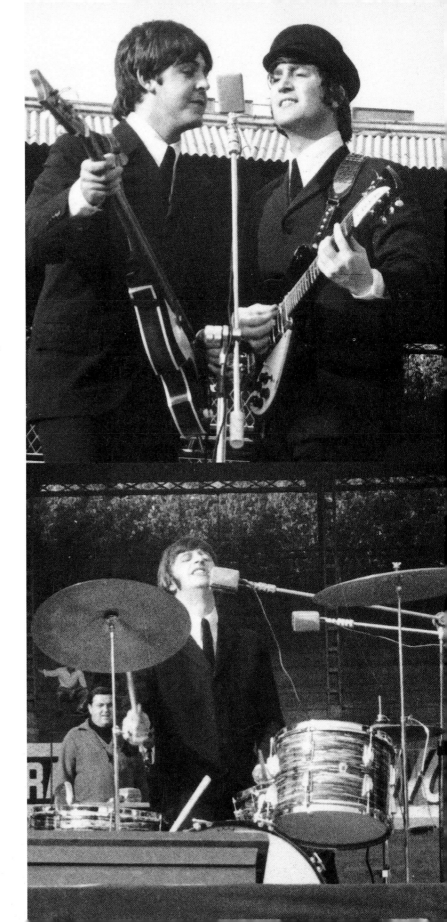

I also took concert shots in Australia. Here Paul fills the room. In this case a relatively small one: the Sydney Boxing Stadium.

Eight Arms to Hold You

This was the original title for *Help!*, which was scripted by Charles Wood though there was initially some talk of having Joe Orton write it. The Beatles had loved the visual idea of eight arms entwined around a young woman. But after 'Help!' was written they had to content themselves with grasping ski poles. The first thing I remember about being on location in Obertauern, in March 1965, is Ringo asking me at dinner on the first night, 'Have you met me missus?' He and Maureen had just married, and this was their extended honeymoon in the snow. Then John added, 'Meet my wife, Cynthia.' 'How do you do,' I replied. 'How do you do,' John echoed. 'How do you do, you do, you do, you do.'

George has always been a keen photographer. He borrowed visitors' cameras to polish his skills whenever he could.

George took pictures. Here Paul takes a different sort of 'shot'.

It was more than thirty years ago today... Though of course, at the time these shots were taken, it would be another two years before Paul wrote 'Sergeant Pepper'. Note George taking a bite out of his cymbal.

Left to right: Cynthia Lennon, Patti Boyd (later Harrison) and Maureen Starkey. Needless to say – given the boys' mock bachelor image – a cameo appearance by any of the 'Beatle wives' in Help! was strictly taboo. The gentleman in the chequered shirt, to the far right, is Roy Kinnear.

Previous spread: *John and Cynthia try out their skis. Paul chats with Australian ski champion Christine Smith, as two* Help! *cast members, Australian actors John Bluthal and Leo 'Rumpole of the Bailey' McKern, mug for the camera.*

Left: *'Long Tall Mally'. The Beatles' devoted road manager, Mal Evans, who'd just emerged from the ice as part of a scene in the film. Sadly, years later Mally was shot and killed by a policeman in the US, after a misunderstanding about a gun.*

George tries out snow curling, assisted by Gigi Mackh, Miss Austria 1964. This was part of a setpiece in Help! *involving a bomb. I was an unpaid skiing extra in the film, though only I can recognize myself running from the explosion in the snow.*

Ringo shovels snow while
the Beatle wives lunch late.

Paul. At right, again with ski champion Christine Smith

***Overleaf:** A collection of Beatle poses. In the upper left-hand corner, Paul skis alongside Neil Aspinall. All 'seven' of the Beatles enjoyed one-upmanship. It was because of Paul's surprise at seeing beginner Neil smoothly skiing past him on the first day that he decided to try out the sport for himself. Recently, Neil was the producer of the out-standing* Beatles Anthology.

Left: *Paul plays his mum and dad rolled into one and even today still wags his finger at a disobedient world.*

Below: *The boys prepare for the toboggan sequence.*

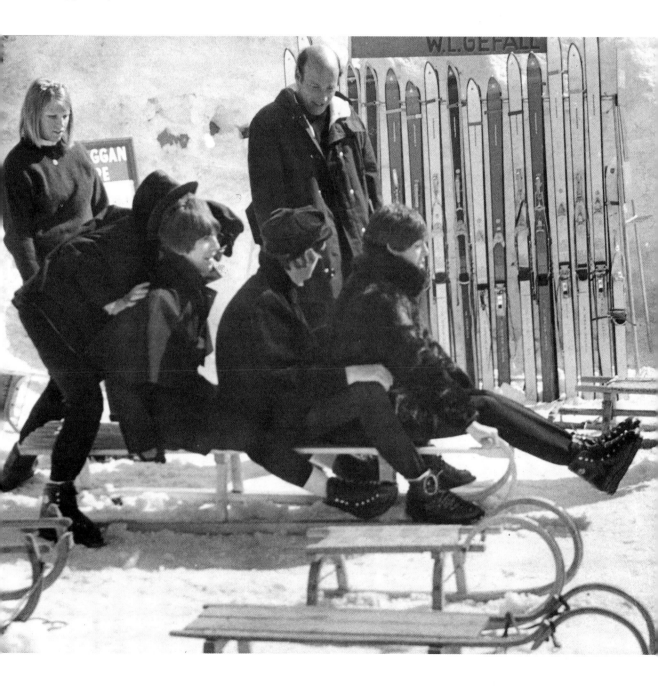

Paul (on my skis!) with Harriet Mary Davidson, the Duke of Norfolk's niece, who after helping Paul with his skiing for half an hour was coupled with him in the press. 'Don't tell anybody about your connections, will you?' Paul asked her when the rumour broke. 'I'm class-conscious, I am.'

John waits patiently as techni-cians confer. Note Harriet Mary Davidson in the foreground.

Above: *The shot is ready. A beaming technician wishes the boys good luck.*

Overleaf: *The result. The hefty figure to the left in the first picture is Mal Evans. The Beatles were doing their own stunt, and* it was Mally's job to tackle his pals as they swooshed down the slope, leaving Ringo's character suspended upside down.

Technically, the Beatles were not supposed to ski for insurance reasons. Needless to say, these regulations were only loosely followed…

Left: Paul with another Help!
principal, Victor Spinetti, here
disguised as an evil snowman.

Right: Paul 'ooh my bum's
numb' McCartney shares a ski
lift with George.

Paul takes basic instruction.
His teachers include Trudy Fox,
who appeared in the 'curling
sequence' of the film.

Overleaf: John and Paul play
in the snow with John Bluthal.

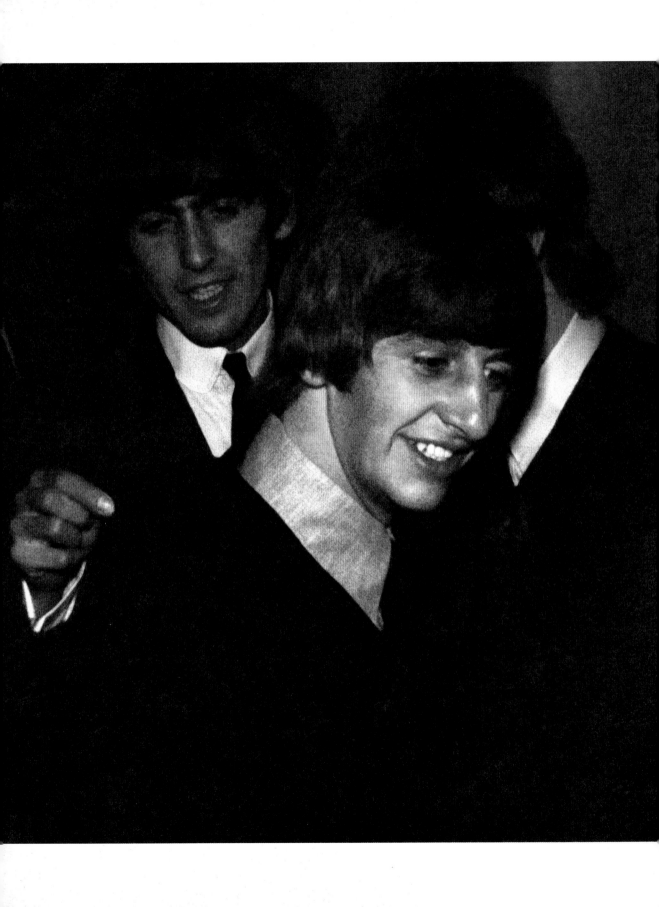

Previous spread: The Beatles depart for New Zealand, carrying with them a giant replica of that country's national emblem, the kiwi bird, a nocturnal creature that can't stand the daylight (which is a bit how the boys look in this picture).

This spread: The first Beatles animal encounter I organized was with a docile blue kangaroo, coincidentally named Cynthia, who was loaned to me by Sir Edward Hallstrom. She was supposed to meet the boys on the plane but at the last minute, when fans broke through security cordons and started running towards the aircraft, police decided it was not safe for Cynthia to 'hop' aboard. In Brisbane though the boys got their wish, when at my party at Lennon's Hotel they met a five-foot kangaroo named Lady Red and a ring-tailed possum named Pierce, who disappeared up Ringo's sleeve later to emerge hanging from one of his fingers. There was also a koala bear named Claude and, of course, the dingo puppy towards which Ringo felt fatherly enough for David Fleay to ask him to christen it 'Ringo' ...

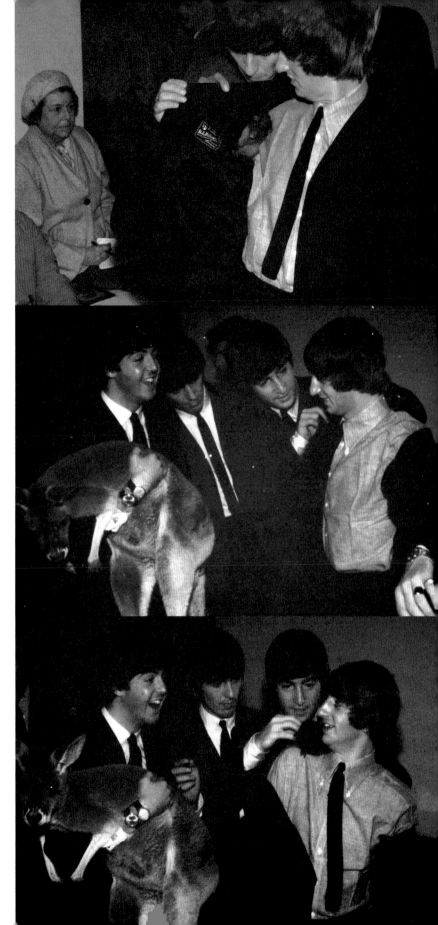

I noticed that while Paul was in Australia he was wearing two watches. He explained to me that one was set for local time and the other for Jane Asher time, so that he could ring his girlfriend in London without waking her.

Above right: John has an extraterrestrial encounter with Lady Red. 'Tie me Lady Red Down, Fred,' he sang in parody of the popular song … 'If Rolf Harris could only see us now,' said George.

Below right: 'Lady Red, you're the best thing since sliced bread,' proclaimed Paul, offering her a slice … 'Has she got a pouch?' asked Ringo … 'Oh there it is. Ringo, don't look!' Paul shouted, and Ringo immediately shut his eyes. Paul was in seventh heaven with Lady Red. 'I love her because she's such a mad animal,' he said. He practically had to be dragged away to make the afternoon concert.

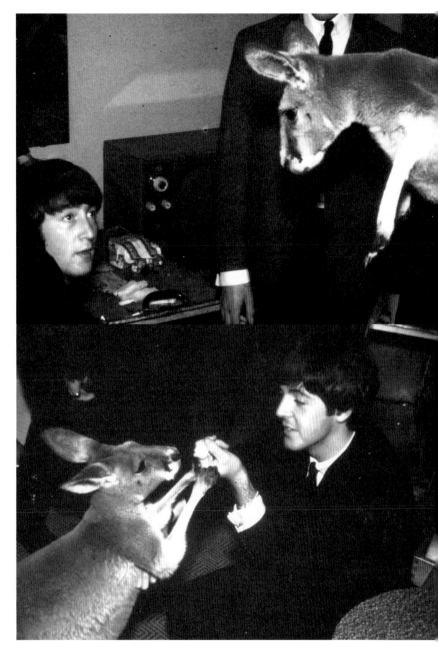

The important women in Ringo's life. *From left, clockwise*: With the former Mrs Starr, Maureen, as a blonde; with Maureen as a brunette; with his second wife, one-time Bond-girl Barbara Bach.

Left: *Ringo dances with chameleon-like Mia Farrow in the Dorchester Ballroom. Mia was a friend of Ringo's wife, Maureen. They shared stories of their recent meditation experiences in India.*

Right: *George with Patti Harrison. Paul with Jane Asher.*

Beatle children. **From left to right:** *Julian Lennon, with his father's guitar. I visited him at his home in Wales soon after John's death. ('The first memory I have of my dad', he told me, 'was when I was a kid and he brought me a birthday cake in the shape of a train with three carriages adorned with candles.'); Linda with her and Paul's younger daughter, the red-headed Stella, who Paul had hoped might be interested in trying out for Annie but who in fact did not make her singing debut until she appeared with the McCartney family singers on a 'say no to drugs' record; Sean Lennon, in the early eighties.*

The last time I saw Yoko Ono,
she and Sean and I were in the
back of a limousine at Heathrow
Airport. I handed her one of my
pictures of John in the desert.
ESP prevailed. At that moment,
Sean was sucking a lollipop.

'Look,' she said, 'John is sucking
a lollipop in the photograph, just
like Sean. John is here with us.'
He is always with us.

A Hard Dazed Knight in the Desert

It was on the strength of his performances in *A Hard Day's Night* and *Help!* that John Lennon was offered the role of Corporal Gripweed in Dick Lester's anti-war satire *How I Won the War*. Lester felt that, of the four, John had the best chance of making it as a character actor in his own right. Filming began in Germany and then moved to the desert location of Almería, Spain, which is where I arranged, through the publicist Brian Rooney, to visit the set in September 1966. As it turned out, this was to be John's only significant non-Beatles film role.

The press made a big fuss over John having to cut his hair short for the film. Here (and in the previous and following pages) he does unto actor and former child star Ron Lacey as was done unto him.

John keeping himself clean-shaven and tidy on the set.

John may have grown restless but he took his role seriously, rehearsing his lines and seeking advice from Ron Lacey and other seasoned actors in the cast.

John mugging with the late Irish character actor Jack MacGowran who played the role of a ventriloquist whose dummy spoke with the voice of Winston Churchill.

A roller was utilized as a comic prop. John and the other 'soldiers' used it to flatten an impromptu cricket pitch.

'Come on! Be in it!' John
pestered Dick Lester, who had
never played cricket before.
'John bowled with such force he
hit my leg and nearly broke it in
two,' Lester later told me. I took
these pictures in the middle of
a dust storm. Even a shutter
speed of one thousandth of a
second was not fast enough to
stop bowler John (see overleaf).
It is Roy Kinnear, by the way,
who is fielding with hands on
his hips in the next spread.

Right: At the time John had a
wonderful habit of curling up
on the ground like a babe in the
womb.

I took these pictures of John with a rifle the day after shooting had begun in Almería. Dick Lester, who was clearly disturbed by the photos when I showed them to him years later, commented, 'John was just messing around. He never fired a rifle in the film.'

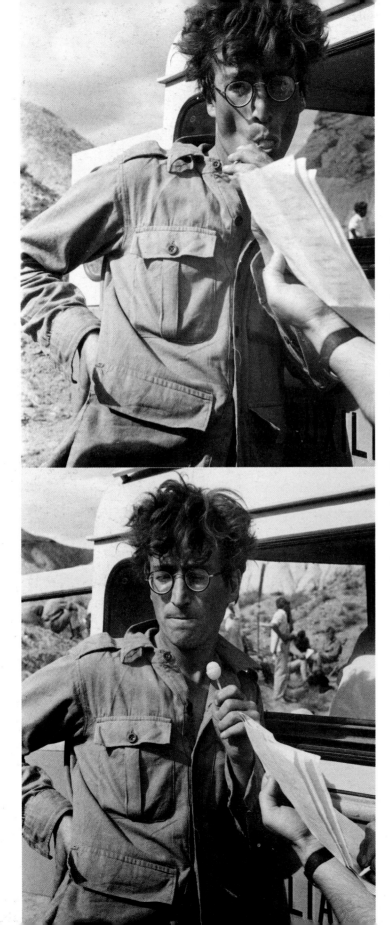

Previous pages: John, again in semi-foetal position, with (from left to right) Jack Hedley, a script girl, Lee Montague and Michael Crawford.

These pages: 'I love these granny glasses that Dick had made up for me on the NHS,' John commented. 'I've been short-sighted since I was ten and I hated those heavy horn-rimmed ones. I'd be so blind that when we'd be on tour and rushing on stage the other lads would say, "John, John, quick, the door on the left," and I'd rush through and find I was holed up by myself in a broom cupboard.'

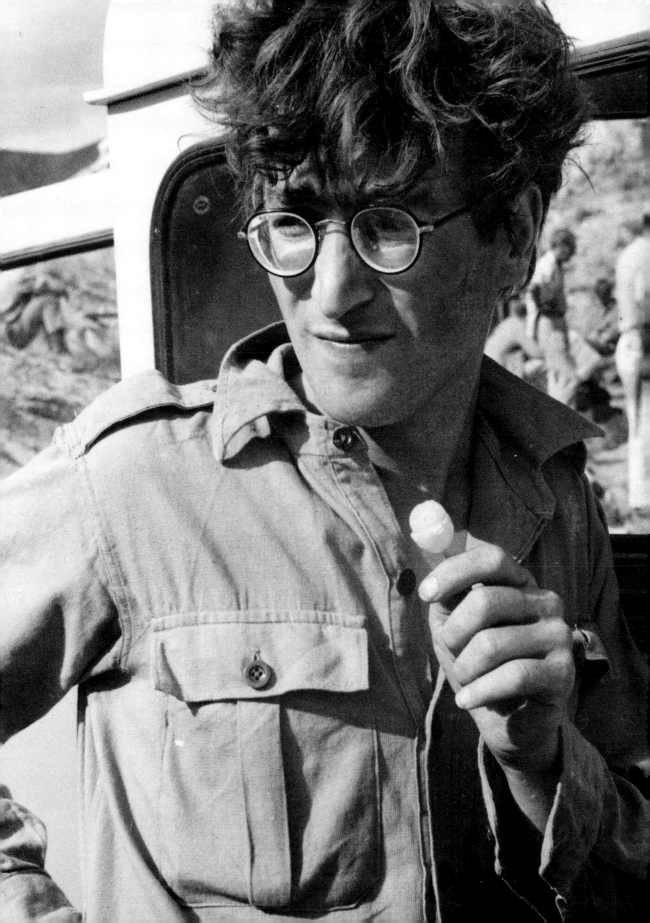

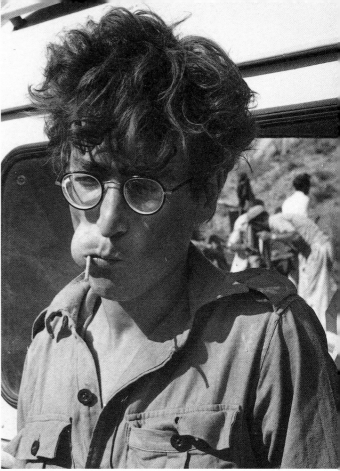
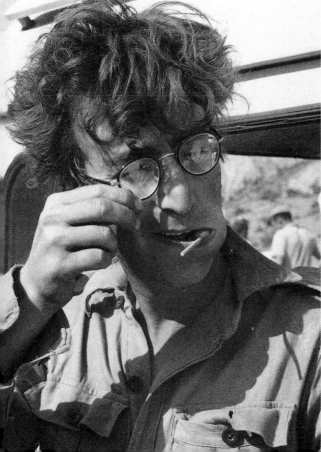

*John takes direction from
his friend and film mentor,
Dick Lester.*

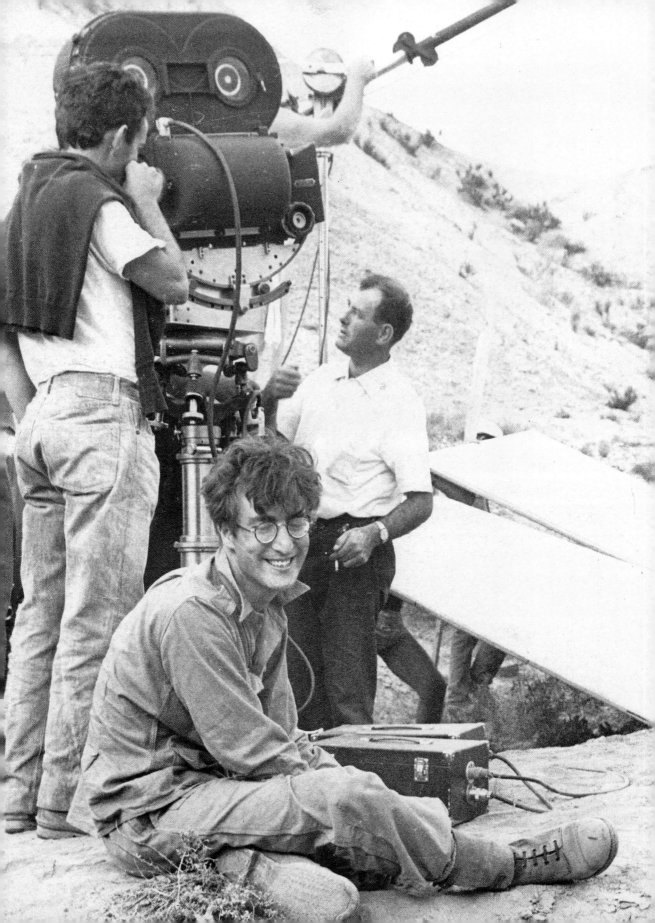

John surprised me with the range of his expressions and his persona on the set. I kept these desert pictures 'on ice' for thirty years, and I'm still startled by some of the images I uncover.

My Leica caught a few drops of water from John's mug. In the movie, as a military batman, he served Michael Crawford tea made from sand and water.

Right: John's performance in a non-musical role was surprisingly polished and precise beside that of his co-star Crawford. Dick Lester, pictured here between the two, enjoyed having John on the set.

Overleaf: These are the two photographs Dick called 'the best pictures that exist of John Lennon'. The first shows an unabashedly childlike John replete with lollipop. The second, though grainy, is probably my own favourite: my 'Fool on the Hill' picture. Paul did not write the song until a year later, but the moment I heard it, I thought of this shot.

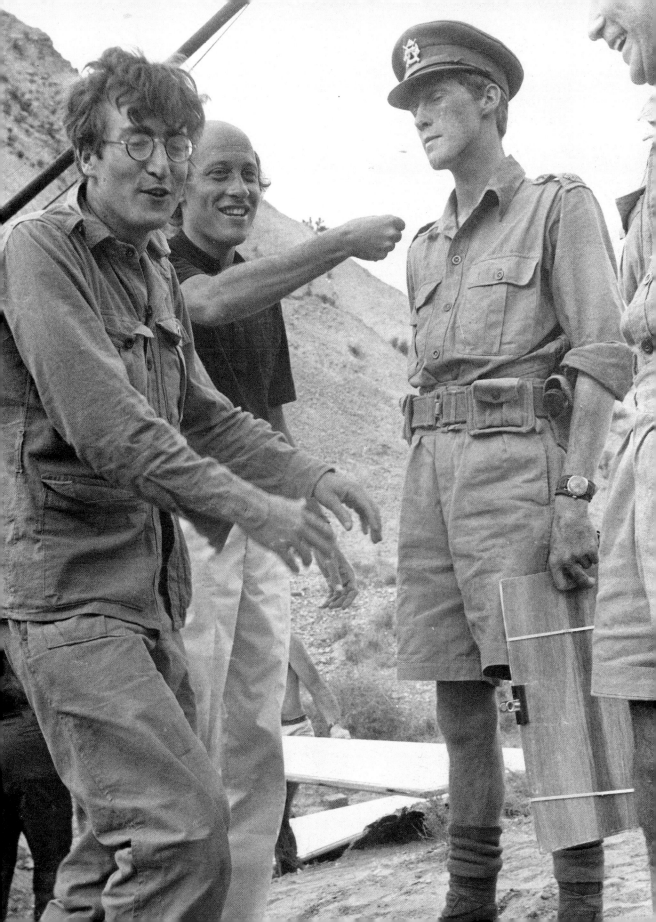

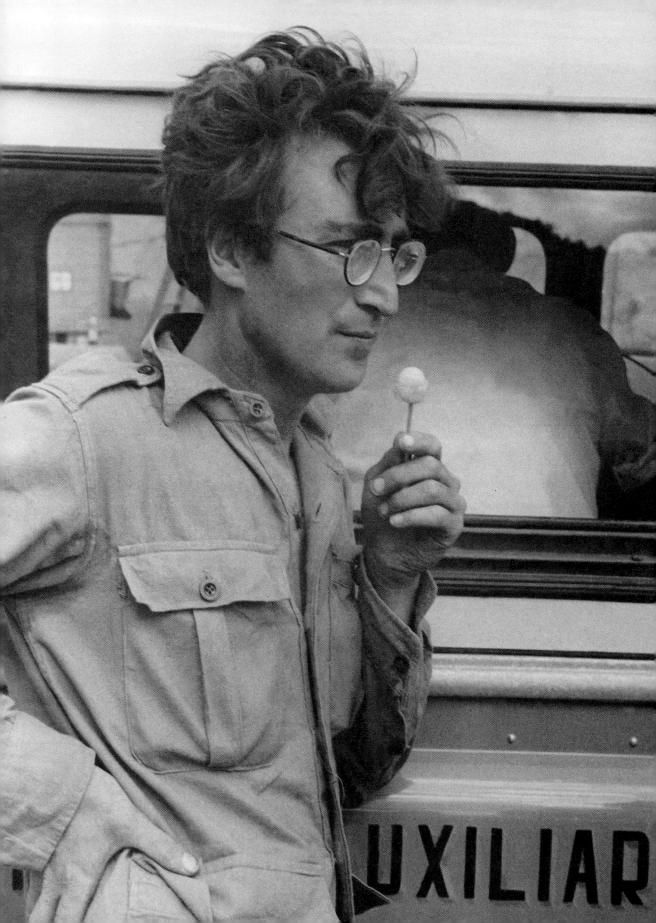

P.S., They Love You

All four of the Beatles seemed to enjoy parties. Paul, especially, was often seen with his actress fiancée, Jane Asher (who was very protective of her own career and, as a rule, did not accompany Paul on film sets; indeed she had her own sets to work on, appearing in films such as *Alfie*, in which she co-starred with Michael Caine). I sometimes flew in for the big premières or launches.

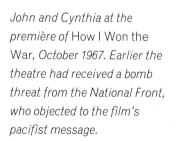

John and Cynthia at the première of How I Won the War, *October 1967. Earlier the theatre had received a bomb threat from the National Front, who objected to the film's pacifist message.*

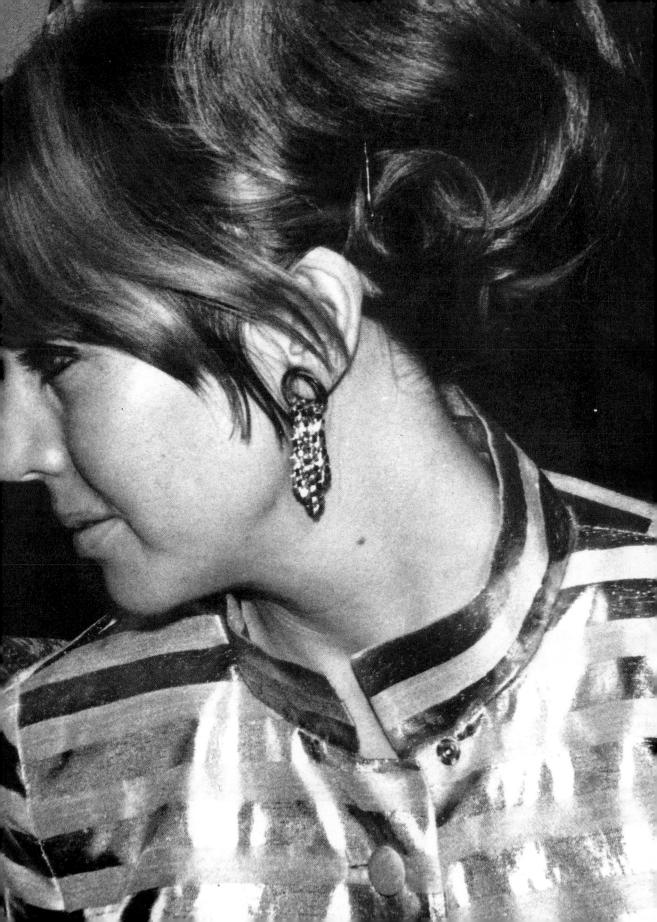

Above: Ringo. Note, entering stage left, Cynthia Lennon and, behind her, Beatles press officer Derek Taylor, whom John immortalized by rhyming his name with 'Norman Mailer' in 'Give Peace a Chance'.

Right: Paul with Jane Asher. It was for Jane that Paul wrote, amongst others, 'And I Love Her', 'She's a Woman', 'I'm Looking through You', 'For No One' and 'Wild Honey Pie'. Jane now makes her own 'honey pies' in her famous cake shop,

and can sometimes be seen on television basting a turkey before millions. On the other hand, the love of Paul's life, his wife for forever and a day, Linda, spends millions trying to stop turkeys from being basted.

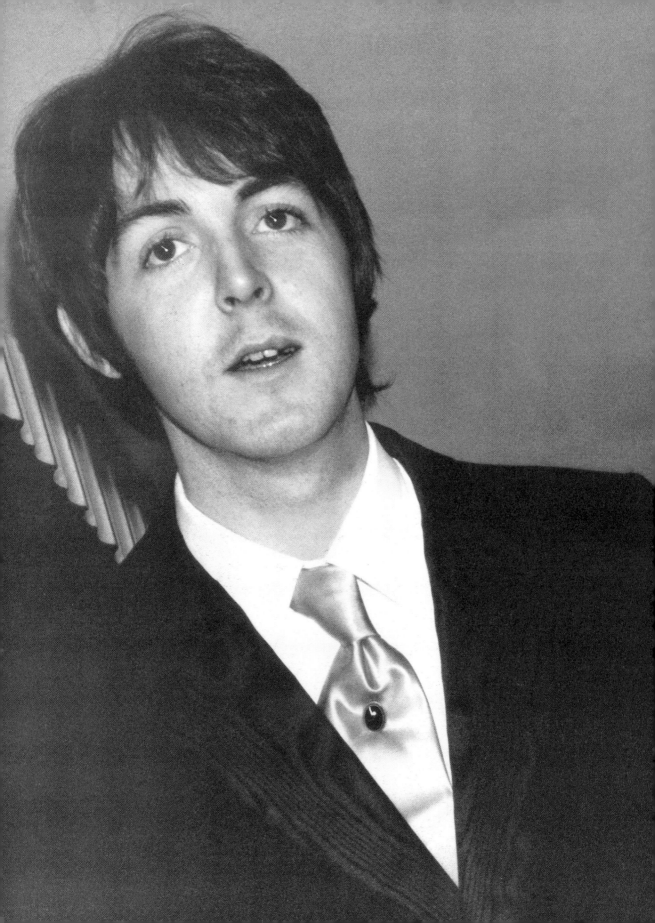

Above: Ringo with a demure Maureen.

Right: Ringo with Ewa Aulin, with whom he starred in 1968's Candy, which marked the beginning of Ringo's non-Beatles film career.

Left: George with the inspirational Patti Boyd. They seemed the ideal showbiz couple until they split. George went on to marry Olivia. Patti, who inspired both 'Something' and 'Layla', married Eric Clapton.

Right and overleaf: Ringo, pictured with Maureen, had to drink for both himself and John and Yoko at the launch of their classic, 'Give Peace a Chance'. Ringo and his wife were standing in for the wild ones, who had been hospitalized after a car accident in Scotland en route to the launch. It took place at the humble Chelsea Town Hall, and there was not a very big turn-out. But Ringo seemed to enjoy himself and I was lucky enough to get some good shots.

April Fools for Peace

One month after my trip to visit him in the desert, John was back in London in search of a change in his life. This occurred in the form of Yoko Ono, whom he met on 9 November in the Indica art gallery, which was owned by Paul's close friend, John Dunbar. I did not meet Yoko until nearly two years later, on 18 July 1968, when John introduced me to her at the première of *Yellow Submarine*. My notes from the time describe her as 'a fragile flower ready to bloom'. John was very proud. This pride also showed when he and Yoko returned to London, on 1 April 1969, after their Gibraltar marriage and Amsterdam bed-in. At the airport John displayed the marriage licence and he and Yoko promoted their 'Plant an Acorn for Peace' campaign, which involved sending acorns to world leaders such as Nixon, Wilson, Trudeau, Satō and Gorton so that they might plant them and the ensuing oak trees would become monuments to peace. 'We are happy to be April fools today,' said John, 'if we are April fools for peace.' Where are they now? (The oak trees, not the leaders!)

*John Lennon, peace will be won someday
it may, someday,
        someday, someday, someday …*